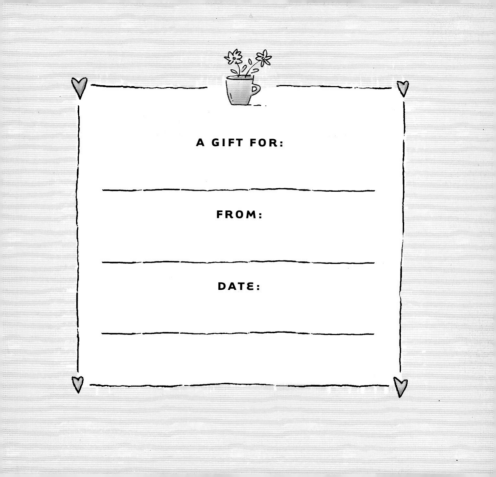

A GIFT FOR:

_____

FROM:

_____

DATE:

_____

Crazy About My Daughter

BARBOUR
PUBLISHING

CRAZY ABOUT MY DAUGHTER™

COPYRIGHT © 2003 BY MARK GILROY COMMUNICATIONS, INC.
TULSA, OKLAHOMA

ART AND DESIGN BY JACKSON DESIGN COMPANY
SILOAM SPRINGS, ARKANSAS

ISBN 1-58660-849-5

SCRIPTURE QUOTATIONS ARE TAKEN FROM THE *HOLY BIBLE,*
NEW LIVING TRANSLATION, COPYRIGHT © 1996. USED BY
PERMISSION OF TYNDALE HOUSE PUBLISHERS, INC.,
WHEATON, ILLINOIS 60189. ALL RIGHTS RESERVED.

PUBLISHED BY BARBOUR PUBLISHING, INC., P.O. BOX 719,
UHRICHSVILLE, OHIO 44683, www.barbourpublishing.com

Member of the
Evangelical Christian
Publishers Association

PRINTED IN CHINA.
5 4 3 2 1

You are God's gift to me!

CHILDREN ARE A GIFT FROM THE LORD;
THEY ARE A REWARD FROM HIM.

PSALM 127:3 NLT

I'M CRAZY ABOUT MY DAUGHTER BECAUSE SHE IS ALWAYS LOOKING FOR WAYS TO SAVE US MONEY.

No W-A-A-A-A-y! What did she say?

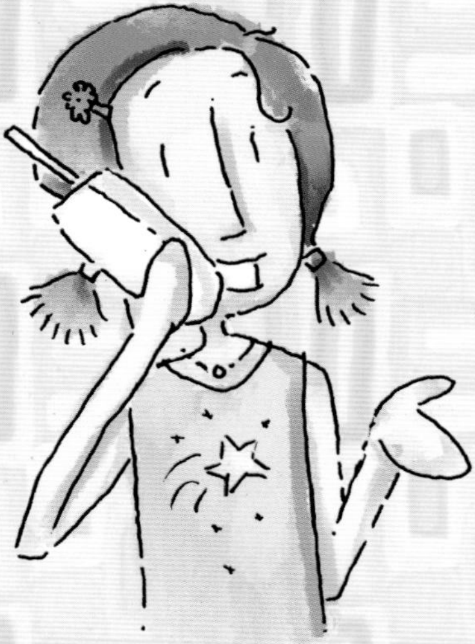

I'M CRAZY ABOUT MY DAUGHTER
BECAUSE SHE STAYS ON TOP
OF CURRENT EVENTS.

I'M CRAZY ABOUT MY DAUGHTER
BECAUSE SHE IS UP ON ALL
THE LATEST BEAUTY TREATMENTS.

I'M CRAZY ABOUT MY DAUGHTER
BECAUSE GIRLS AREN'T NEARLY
AS LOUD AS BOYS.

I'M CRAZY ABOUT MY DAUGHTER
BECAUSE SHE ALWAYS HAS
HER ROOM LOOKING GREAT.

I'M CRAZY ABOUT MY DAUGHTER
BECAUSE SHE WAKES UP
WITH A SMILE ON HER FACE.

I'M CRAZY ABOUT MY DAUGHTER BECAUSE
SHE LAUGHS AT ALL DAD'S JOKES.

I'M CRAZY ABOUT MY DAUGHTER
BECAUSE SHE IS SO LADYLIKE.

I'M CRAZY ABOUT MY DAUGHTER
BECAUSE SHE TAKES THE TIME TO LOOK
HER VERY BEST IN THE MORNING.

I'M CRAZY ABOUT MY DAUGHTER BECAUSE
OF HER AMAZING ABILITY TO MULTITASK.

I'M CRAZY ABOUT MY DAUGHTER
BECAUSE I'M SURE SHE WON'T MIND
MY RULE THAT SHE CAN'T DATE
UNTIL SHE IS 30 YEARS OLD.

I'M CRAZY ABOUT MY DAUGHTER
BECAUSE SHE'S ALWAYS ON
THE CUTTING EDGE OF FASHION.

(SOMETIMES MOM THINKS SHE'S
A LITTLE OVER THE EDGE.)

I'M CRAZY ABOUT MY DAUGHTER
BECAUSE SHE IS SUCH A HEALTHY EATER.

I'M CRAZY ABOUT MY DAUGHTER
BECAUSE SHE IS KIND AND
CONSIDERATE AND ALWAYS
ANSWERS THE PHONE FOR US.

I'M CRAZY ABOUT MY DAUGHTER
BECAUSE SHE HAS A GO-FOR-IT SPIRIT.

I'M CRAZY ABOUT MY DAUGHTER
BECAUSE SHE LOVES SPENDING
QUALITY TIME WITH HER MOTHER.

I'M CRAZY ABOUT MY DAUGHTER
BECAUSE SHE DOESN'T LET LITTLE THINGS
LIKE A BAD HAIR DAY GET HER DOWN.

I'M CRAZY ABOUT MY DAUGHTER BECAUSE
SHE HAS THE VIRTUE OF PERSISTENCE.

I'M CRAZY ABOUT MY DAUGHTER
BECAUSE SHE WAS A NATURAL ATHLETE
FROM THE VERY START.

I'M CRAZY ABOUT MY DAUGHTER
BECAUSE SHE'S ALWAYS READY
WHEN THE CAMERA IS.

I'M CRAZY ABOUT MY DAUGHTER
BECAUSE SHE HAS MASTERED
THE FINE ART OF PERSUASION.

I'M CRAZY ABOUT MY DAUGHTER
BECAUSE SHE ENJOYS ALL KINDS
OF MUSIC ～ EVEN DAD'S.

I'M CRAZY ABOUT MY DAUGHTER
BECAUSE SHE HAS AN INCREDIBLE SENSE
OF LOYALTY TO HER CLOSE FRIENDS.

I'M CRAZY ABOUT MY DAUGHTER
BECAUSE SHE IS ALWAYS PROUD TO BE
SEEN IN PUBLIC WITH HER FAMILY

(OR AT LEAST USUALLY).

I'M CRAZY ABOUT MY DAUGHTER
BECAUSE SHE REALLY GETS
INTO THE CHRISTMAS SPIRIT.

I'M CRAZY ABOUT MY DAUGHTER
BECAUSE SHE ALWAYS PLANS AHEAD.

I'M CRAZY ABOUT MY DAUGHTER BECAUSE OF HER LOVE FOR THE GREAT OUTDOORS.

I'M CRAZY ABOUT MY DAUGHTER
BECAUSE SHE IS ALREADY GIFTED
IN THE CULINARY ARTS.

I'M CRAZY ABOUT MY DAUGHTER
BECAUSE SHE GETS ALONG SO WELL
WITH HER BROTHER.

yes, your brother has chores he has to do, too.

I'M CRAZY ABOUT MY DAUGHTER
BECAUSE SHE IS ALWAYS READY
TO HELP AROUND THE HOUSE

(AND NEVER COMPLAINS).

I'M CRAZY ABOUT MY DAUGHTER
BECAUSE SHE REMINDS ME OF HER MOM.

I'M CRAZY ABOUT MY DAUGHTER
BECAUSE SHE'S ALWAYS EAGER
AND READY FOR FAMILY VACATION.

I'M CRAZY ABOUT MY DAUGHTER
BECAUSE SHE'S EASY TO SHOP FOR.

If you need any other ideas, I can add more.

Oh, Aunt Thelma, thank you SO much.

I'M CRAZY ABOUT MY DAUGHTER
BECAUSE SHE HAS THE SPIRIT
OF APPRECIATION.

I'M CRAZY ABOUT MY DAUGHTER
BECAUSE SHE EATS A BALANCED DIET
WITH ALL FIVE FOOD GROUPS

(INCLUDING CHOCOLATE).

I'M CRAZY ABOUT MY DAUGHTER
BECAUSE SHE'S SO PRETTY THAT SHE
ALWAYS STANDS OUT IN A CROWD.

I'M CRAZY ABOUT MY DAUGHTER
BECAUSE SHE'S BRAVE AND CONFIDENT.

(EXCEPT FOR THUNDERSTORM NIGHTS!)

I'M CRAZY ABOUT MY DAUGHTER BECAUSE
SHE KNOWS RIGHT FROM WRONG.

I'M CRAZY ABOUT MY DAUGHTER BECAUSE
SHE TRULY DOES HAVE A KIND HEART.

I'M CRAZY ABOUT MY DAUGHTER
BECAUSE NO MATTER HOW OLD SHE GETS,
SHE'LL ALWAYS BE MY LITTLE GIRL.

I'M CRAZY ABOUT MY DAUGHTER BECAUSE SHE KNOWS WHERE TO TURN FOR HELP.

I'M CRAZY ABOUT MY DAUGHTER BECAUSE
SHE ISN'T AFRAID OF A CHALLENGE.

I'M CRAZY ABOUT MY DAUGHTER
BECAUSE SHE KNOWS HOW TO LET ME
KNOW HOW MUCH SHE LOVES ME.

I'M CRAZY ABOUT MY DAUGHTER BECAUSE
I'VE PRAYED FOR HER EVERY DAY.

I'M CRAZY ABOUT MY DAUGHTER
BECAUSE SHE TRULY IS BECOMING
A BEAUTIFUL YOUNG WOMAN.